Pillow Thoughts

Shawna Bomberger

BookLeaf Publishing

Presentation by *BookLeaf Publishing*

Web: www.bookleafpub.com

E-mail: info@bookleafpub.com

ISBN: 9789358369076

First edition 2023

New Beginnings

A new beginning, a fresh start.
Excitement flutters the heart.
A new page, with all that blankness.
A new journey could feel anxious.
A new job, a new town,
With some time, you'll figure it out.
To start a new journey, it's never too late.
Everyday is a fresh start, to do something great.

Trust the Process

Trust the process
Because little by little
Will come the progress
Believe it can happen
But don't be slackin'
It will get trying
But if you keep pushing
There will be no denying
With one life to live
Eventually it will give
Trust the process
Eventually you will progress

Heart in Disguise

Life with you felt meant to be.
It was you and me, then came three.
I gave you my all, gave you my time.
How it felt to look deep in your eyes.
Like transferring my love into your soul.
The feeling of a heart that's whole.
You left and now my world's a wreck.
Life is lonely, no one keeping in check.
Your words and actions left their scars,
So I'll build these walls, keep up my guard.
"All is well", I'm acting fine.
Just a broken heart in disguise.

Toxic Love

Like a knife, his words cut deep.
Generational trauma she won't repeat.
The pain feels familiar.
What love must be, she figures.
It could've been forever.
But love should feel better.
It's too hard to say goodbye.
The good times feel so high.
The good times, she's weak in the knees.
The bad times, are hard to believe.
The love feels intoxicating.
Leaving feels more complicated.
This isn't love, it's toxic.
Leave, before it makes you sick.

Stone Heart

Who can I trust in a world so cold?
To have my heart and to hold.
He said he loved me, I felt like home.
So why do I feel so alone?
With those wandering eyes,
And his foolish lies,
It's no surprise my guard is high.
My mind can't erase the things he said.
And if "actions speak louder than words"
Does that mean he's dead?
But when it's hard to trust,
The heart collects dust.
If someone could ever get this wall down,
Then maybe true love could be found.

Spilt Milk

She isn't crying over spilt milk.
Even though it's on her favorite quilt.
She's been overwhelmed and stretched thin.
She'd ask for help, but where would she begin?
She's losing herself, she's missing her friends.
But things keep coming up, it never ends.
All the housework and meals to cook.
Piles of laundry, reading the kids a book.
She no longer cares about how she looks.
It's been so long since she's felt loved.
One soft kiss would have her buzzed.
Finding balance in life, how does one handle?
All these things may seem insubstantial.
But overtime, when stress has built.
It's easy to cry over spilt milk.

Motivation

Motivation isn't something you find.
Motivation is too complex to describe.
It's a feeling deep within the soul.
It's more than desire to achieve a goal.
Motivation doesn't always feel pleasing.
But it's the only way to keep achieving.

Everybody Love Everybody

When you see a man begging for money,
I hope you see that he's still somebody.
We are all the same.
It could be you some day.
Life has no guarantees.
Open your eyes and you will see.
We all have troubles,
Even if they aren't the same struggles.
When you can, lend a hand.
Try to understand.
Compassion for others.
You never know their hardest struggles.

Lost Connection

All they care about are the likes and follows.
Nevermind how that makes a heart feel hollow.
So much as been lost, not being in the present.
The simple times of being an adolescent.
It's like we forgot how to look in someone's
eyes.
Behind the keyboard, could be so many lies.
With all the filters, who can you trust?
Such a fast pace world, how do you adjust?

Lemonade

When life gives you lemons, what can you do?
You can save them for a rainy day.
You can throw them out or give them away.
You can add them to your water,
Or wait around for a better offer.
But the reality of life,
Is there's not a lot of lemons to be given.
Life will give you loss and grieving.
Losing loved ones is anything but pleasing.
Life will disappoint you.
It won't always play out how you want to.
So when life has a lemon to spare,
Don't take it for granted,
Don't you dare!
When life gives you lemons,
Just enjoy some lemonade.

Imprisoned Love

If loving you is wrong, I don't wanna be right.
Loving you was wrong, let's bring it to light.
How could you see the true me,
When all you wanted was to screw me?
You were never on my team.
You never cared about my dreams.
I fell for your lies.
I ignored the signs.
But for the last time.
Because like a crime,
Life without parole.
I'll never let in another soul.
Lesson learned. Now I got it right.
Only a fool believes in love at first sight.

Stolen Heart

Like a thief in the night, you stole my heart.
Was your charm genuine, or was it an art?
You stole my heart, the parts you wanted.
You stole my love, left me broken-hearted.
Love doesn't come with insurance policies.
But I would've settled for sincere apologies.

You're Late, Soulmate

When you know, you know.
It's that kind of love that continues to grow.
He's your best friend, you talk about everything.
He's means more to you than just a fling.
Feeling your heartbeat in places you wont admit.
He's the kind of man who will commit.
To feel desired,
Or simply admired.
For better or worse,
Just kiss me 'til it hurts.
When you know, you know.
But when will he show?

Tell Them You Love Them

The days can drag but the years go fast.
Life doesn't warn you, how long it will last.
How we can't control the clouds in the sky,
We can't control how life passes by.
Sometimes we lose people, and it won't make
sense.
So tell them you love them, before the time is
past-tense.

Terra

I remember the words, I feel the tone.
The devastating news coming through the
phone.
My mind couldn't grasp how it could've been
you.
How much pain you must have gone through.
We were best friends, told each other everything.
I thought you could come to me about anything.
I refused to hear how it happened.
I kept my feelings trapped in.
Part of me, felt to blame.
Part of me, wanted to do the same.
Living life without your best friend,
Is a lot of time spent, trying to pretend.
Years go by, and I still have to lie.
Whenever they ask, I tell them I'm fine.
But I still wince at the word "suicide."
Will the sadness ever go away?
Time will heal, is what they say.

Mom's Magic

A home cooked meal fills the kitchen.
Always part of Momma's Christmas tradition.
For us, she always went above and beyond.
I swear, she had help with a magic wand.
She had a way of making each child feel
treasured.
Her love for her kids is unmeasured.
The sacrifices she made, just to survive.
Thank you mom, for keeping the magic alive.

Peanut Butter Paintings

From the day you were born, it all made sense.
I never knew a love could be so intense.
You're tiny fingers would wrap around mine,
You're precious laughs had me on cloud nine.
They try to tell us how fast kids grow,
But until they're your own, it's hard to know.
Soon, the toys take over the house.
All we watch is Mickey Mouse.
Somehow lunch has splattered the walls.
But the joy you get, being chased down the
halls.
Nothing compares to seeing your smile.
I feel so blessed to call you my child.
One day I'll be wishing you were this small.
One day I'll be missing your peanut butter
paintings on the wall.

Jaxson

My son,
My sweet boy.
Because of you, I've felt real joy.
The way I feel when I'm with you,
Is worth hard times I had to go through.
I love how you trust me when you're hurt.
How you love me, even at my worst.
I love how you come to me, running.
How can someone be so loving?
You are my proudest creation.
You are my motivation.
To do my best for you.
If you only knew,
How much I love you